AF481443

# Contents

## INTRODUCTION

Collagen is the most abundant protein in your body, accounting for about a third of its protein composition.

It's one of the major building blocks of bones, skin, muscles, tendons, and ligaments. Collagen is also found in many other body parts, including blood vessels, corneas, and teeth.

You can think of it as the "glue" that holds all these things together. In fact, the word comes from the Greek word "kólla," which means glue.

Collagen is the most plentiful protein in the body.

It has important roles, including providing

structure to your skin and helping your blood

clot.

In recent years, it's gained popularity as a

nutritional supplement and ingredient in

shampoos and body lotions.

Supplementing with collagen daily can improve

skin hydration, fine lines, and overall appearance

of skin. It also supports the growth of hair and

nails. Maintains a healthy gut barrier and

supports good digestion. Glutamine and glycine,

two amino acids abundant in collagen, are

essential for healthy digestion.

## WHAT IS COLLAGEN?

Collagen is the most abundant protein in your body, accounting for about a third of its protein composition.

It's one of the major building blocks of bones, skin, muscles, tendons, and ligaments. Collagen is also found in many other body parts, including blood vessels, corneas, and teeth.

You can think of it as the "glue" that holds all these things together. In fact, the word comes from the Greek word "kólla," which means glue.

There are at least 16 types of collagen. The four main types are type I, II, III, and IV

Here's a closer look at the four main types of collagen and their role in your body:

• Type I: This type accounts for 90% of your body's collagen and is made of densely packed fibers. It provides structure to skin, bones, tendons, fibrous cartilage, connective tissue, and teeth.

• Type II: This type is made of more loosely packed fibers and is found in elastic cartilage, which cushions joints.

• Type III: This type supports the structure of muscles, organs, and arteries.

• Type IV: This type helps with filtration and is found in layers of your skin.

As you age, your body produces less and lower-quality collagen.

One of the visible signs of this is in your skin, which becomes less firm and supple. Cartilage also weakens with age.

## NUTRIENTS THAT INCREASE COLLAGEN PRODUCTION

All collagen starts off as procollagen.

Your body makes procollagen by combining two amino acids: glycine and proline. This process uses vitamin C.

You may be able to help your body produce this important protein by making sure you get plenty of the following nutrients:

• Vitamin C: Large amounts are found in citrus fruits, bell peppers, and strawberries.

• Proline: Large amounts are found in egg whites, wheat germ, dairy products, cabbage, asparagus, and mushrooms.

• Glycine: Large amounts are found in pork skin, chicken skin, and gelatin, but glycine is also found in various protein-containing foods.

• Copper: Large amounts are found in organ meats, sesame seeds, cocoa powder, cashews, and lentils.

In addition, your body needs high quality protein that contains the amino acids needed to make new proteins. Meat, poultry, seafood, dairy, legumes, and tofu are all excellent sources of amino acids.

## THINGS THAT DAMAGE COLLAGEN

Perhaps it's even more important to avoid the following collagen-destroying behaviors:

• Sugar and refined carbs: Sugar interferes with collagen's ability to repair itself. Minimize your consumption of added sugar and refined carbs.

• Too much sunshine: Ultraviolet radiation can reduce collagen production. Avoid excessive sun exposure.

• Smoking: Smoking reduces collagen production. This can impair wound healing and lead to wrinkles.

Some autoimmune disorders, such as lupus, can also damage collagen.

Collagen is found in the connective tissues of animal foods. For example, it's found in large amounts in chicken and pork skin.

One particularly rich source is bone broth, which is made by boiling down the bones of chicken and other animals.

Gelatin is basically cooked collagen, so it's very high in the amino acids needed to produce it.

But there's debate over whether consuming collagen-rich foods actually increases the levels in your body.

When you eat protein, it's broken down into amino acids and then reassembled, so the collagen you eat wouldn't translate directly into higher levels in your body.



Two types supplements are gaining popularity: hydrolyzed collagen (collagen hydrolysate) and gelatin. Gelatin is created when collagen is cooked.

These have already broken the large protein down into smaller peptides, which are more easily absorbed in the body.

There aren't many studies on collagen supplements, but those that exist show promise for benefits in the following areas:

• Muscle mass: A 2019 study in recreationally

active men showed that a combination of

collagen peptide supplements and strength

training increased muscle mass and strength

more than a placebo.

• Arthritis: A 2017 animal study looked at the

effects of giving collagen supplements to mice

with post-traumatic osteoarthritis (PTOA). The

results indicated that supplementation may play

a protective role in the disease's development

and progression.

• Skin elasticity: Women who took a supplement

showed improvements in skin appearance and

elasticity in a 2019 study. Collagen is also used in

topical treatments to improve the appearance of

skin by minimizing lines and wrinkle.

Some alternative medicine practitioners also

advocate using collagen supplements to treat

leaky gut syndrome.


## SAFETY AND SIDE EFFECTS

So far, there's limited reliable information

available on the safety and efficacy of collagen

supplements.

The potential side effects of gelatin supplements

include a lingering unpleasant taste and

sensations of heaviness and heartburn.

Also, if you're allergic to the source of the supplement, you could have an allergic reaction.

## HOW TO SUPPLEMENT

Collagen peptide comes in a powder that can be easily incorporated into foods.

The peptide form doesn't gel, so you can mix it into smoothies, soups, or baked goods without affecting the texture.

You can use gelatin to make homemade jello or gummies.

When considering supplements, you should look for a high quality source. Marine collagen, which is made from fish skin, is also available.

You can find supplements in pill or powder form.

The powder can be easily added to food.


## OTHER USES

Collagen has many uses, from food to medication

to manufacturing.

For thousands of years, collagen was used to

create glue. Today, it's still used to create strings

for musical instruments.

In food, collagen is heated to create gelatin and

used to make casings for sausages. In the medical

field, it's used as a filler in plastic surgery and as a

dressing for severe burns.

Collagen has many uses, including as a dressing

on burns and in making strings for musical

instruments.


## COLLAGEN SMOOTHIES

### KETO COLLAGEN PEPTIDE SMOOTHIE

**Ingredients**

- ¼ large avocado

- 1 ½ tsp chia seeds

- 1 tbsp cocoa powder

- 1 scoop (1/3 oz) collagen peptides

- 1 tbsp almond butter

- ½ cup unsweetened almond milk

- ½ cup water

- liquid stevia to taste (optional)

- ¼– ½ cup ice

## Instructions

- Place all the ingredients in a blender and blend until smooth.

- Serve immediately.

# VANILLA CHAI COLLAGEN PROTEIN SMOOTHIE

## INGREDIENTS

- 2 frozen bananas

- ¾ cup almond milk

- 1 teaspoon vanilla extract

- ¼ teaspoon ground cinnamon

- ¼ teaspoon ground ginger

- ⅛ teaspoon ground cardamom

- ⅛ teaspoon ground cloves

- 2 heaping tablespoons (2 scoops) Further

  Food Collagen

## INSTRUCTIONS

1. Place all ingredients in blender and blend until

smooth and creamy!

## PEACH MATCHA COLLAGEN SMOOTHIE

### Ingredients

- 1 cup unsweetened almond milk

- 1/2 cup frozen peach slices

- 2 scoops Vital Proteins Peach Matcha Collagen

- 1/2 medium avocado

- 2 tsp raw honey

Instructions

- Combine the almond milk, frozen peach slices, Matcha Collagen, avocado and honey in a high-speed blender.

- Process on high until ingredients are combined (about 45 seconds). Serve immediately.

# STRAWBERRY WATERMELON COLLAGEN SMOOTHIE

## Ingredients

- 1 cup pure orange juice, unsweetened

- 1 cup strawberries fresh or frozen

- 1 cup watermelon cubes frozen

- 1/4 cup collagen powder

## Instructions

- Blend all ingredients in a blender until smooth. Divide equally between 2 glasses and serve.

# QUICK COLLAGEN SMOOTHIE WITH CHERRY ROSE

## Ingredients

- 1 Scoop Skinny Fit SUPER YOUTH Collagen
- 1/2 Cup Cherries - pitted
- 1/4 Cup Almonds
- 1/2 Tsp Rose Water or Edible Dried Rose Leaves
- Base of Choice (Use Yogurt/Milk/Vegan Options).

## Instructions

- Add all the ingredients in a blender jar and blend to a smooth mix.

- Transfer to a glass and decorate with dried edible rose petals, sliced cherry, slivered almonds and chocolate syrup.

- Enjoy Cold

## COLLAGEN TROPICAL SMOOTHIE

### INGREDIENTS

- 1 frozen banana

- 1 1/2 cup fresh strawberries

- 1/2 cup orange juice

- 1 teaspoon chia seeds

- 1 scoop collagen peptides

- 2 sprinkles cinnamon

- 1/2 teaspoon shredded coconut

- Place all ingredients in blender and process on high until smooth.

- Pour into 2 glasses. Sprinkle the tops of each smoothie with cinnamon and shredded coconut.



- You can substitute collagen peptides with protein powder for a delicious protein smoothie

## COLLAGEN PROTEIN SMOOTHIE PACKS

### INGREDIENTS

- 1 cup blueberries

- 1 cup spinach or other leafy greens

- 1 tsp grated gingers or 1/4 tsp ground

  ginger

- 1/2 c grapefruit (peeled)

- 1/2 c to 2/3 c pineapple chunks

- 1 tbsp chia seed

- 3 frozen coconut milk ice cubes (coconut

  milk frozen)

- 1 scoop Collage Protein or Peptides – we

  used a Vanilla Coconut Flavor

- Optional – 1/2 c to 1 cup water to blend

DIRECTIONS

- Blend all till smooth

# ENERGIZING PROTEIN SMOOTHIE PACKS



- 1 tbsp unsweetened cocoa or cocao powder

- 1/2 cup almond milk

- 1 –2 servings protein (collagen peptides)

- 2 tbsp peanut butter or almond butter (frozen)

- 1 banana

- 1/4 c gluten free oats

- 1–2 tbsp flaxseed

- Optional – 1/2 c to 1 cup water or almond milk to blend

Directions

- Blend till smooth

# BEAUTIFY PROTEIN SMOOTHIE PACKS

Ingredients

- 1 kiwi

- 1 c raspberries

- 1/2 small avocado (peeled)

- 1 tbsp honey (optional)

- 2–3 frozen coconut milk cubes (from ice tray)

- Lavender Lemon Beauty Collagen Protein (mixed into coconut milk cubes or to add separate)

- Optional – 1/2 c to 1 cup water or almond milk to blend

INSTRUCTIONS

- Blend till smooth

## COFFEE, CACAO AND COLLAGEN SMOOTHIE

INGREDIENTS

- 6 ounces cold brew coffee
- 4 ounces nut milk, we used cashew milk
- 1/2 Tablespoon of cacao powder
- 2 Tablespoons collagen peptides
- 1 Tablespoons MCT oil
- 1 Tablespoon powdered peanut butter
- 1/2 frozen banana

- Pour the coffee and nut milk in the blender first, then add the other ingredients and process until all is smooth and enjoy!



- If you want a thicker smoothie, add in a small handful of ice cubes.

## COFFEE PROTEIN SMOOTHIE

Ingredients

- 1 medium frozen banana (112 gram)

- 1 cup frozen cauliflower rice (100 grams)

- 1 tablespoon cashew butter

- 1 tablespoon chia seeds

- 2 scoops Vital Protein Madagascar Vanilla Collagen Latte

- 1/2 teaspoon cinnamon

- 1 cup cold brew coffee

## Instructions

- All all ingredients to a Vitamix or high powdered blender and blend until smooth, about 1 minute. Top with toppings or drink as it.

# BLUEBERRY COLLAGEN SMOOTHIE (GLOWING SKIN!)

## INGREDIENTS

- 1 cup Coconut Water
- 1 scoop Vital Proteins Collagen Peptides Powder
- 1 handful Blueberries
- 1 frozen Banana
- 1 Tbs Cashew Butter

## INSTRUCTIONS

- Add all ingredients to a high speed blender and blend for 30 seconds until smooth and creamy.
- Enjoy!

# GREEN PROTEIN SMOOTHIE

## Ingredients

- 2 cups baby spinach

- 1 medium apple (cored)

- 1/2 medium banana

- 1/4 avocado

- 2 scoops Vital Proteins Collagen

- 2 inch piece ginger root

- 2 tablespoons lemon juice (about half a lemon)

- 1 tablespoon flax seed meal

- pinch cayenne (optional)

- 1 teaspoon termeric

- ice to taste

- chia seeds and hemp seeds (optional garnish for texture)

## Directions

- Place all ingredients in a high speed blender and puree until smooth. Pour into glads and enjoy

# STRAWBERRY COLLAGEN SMOOTHIE

## Ingredients

- 2 cups unsweetened full fat coconut milk

- 2 cups frozen strawberries

- 2 T raw honey

- 2 T Bright Naturals Collagen

- Combine ingredients in a blender and pulse on high speed until thick and creamy, about 30 seconds.

- Divide between two glasses and serve right away.

## BLUEBERRY COLLAGEN SMOOTHIE

### INGREDIENTS

- 1 cup blueberries

- 1/2 frozen banana **

- 1/2 ripe avocado

- 1 tbsp almond butter

- 1 tbsp chia seeds

- 2 scoops of collagen powder (20 grams of collagen)

- 1 and 1/2 cups milk of any kind or water (I use THIS)

- 1 cup ice – optional



- Combine all ingredients in a blender and process until creamy smooth.

- Enjoy!

## BANANA BERRY SMOOTHIE

### INGREDIENTS

- 1/2 small banana, frozen

- 3/4 cup mixed berries, frozen

- 1 handful of spinach (optional)

- 1 Tbsp. almond butter or nut butter of choice

- 1/4 avocado

- 1 tsp. chia or flax seeds

- 2 scoops collagen peptides or protein of choice

- 1/2–1 cup unsweetened almond milk or milk of choice

- 1/2 cup ice

- optional – 1/2 cup Greek yogurt (omit for dairy-free or vegan)

## INSTRUCTIONS

- Place ingredients in a high-powered blender and blend until smooth. For a thinner smoothie add 1 cup of liquid for a

thicker smoothie start with a 1/2 cup and

add more until desired consistency is

achieved.

## CHOCOLATE COLLAGEN SMOOTHIE

### INGREDIENTS

- 2 cups coconut milk, or other milk

- 1 frozen banana

- 2 tbsp almond butter

- 1/4 cup raw cacao powder

- 2 scoops, or more Vital Proteins Collagen

  Peptides

- Add all ingredients to a high-powered blender and blend until smooth.


## CHOCOLATE COLLAGEN SMOOTHIE

### Ingredients

- 1 scoop Further Foods Chocolate Collagen

- ¼ cup unsweetened almond milk

- 2 tablespoons heavy cream (or more almond milk)

- 1 cup crushed ice

- Few drops chocolate stevia

- Place all the ingredients into a blender and puree until smooth.

- Taste and adjust sweetness to your liking. Pour into a glass and enjoy!

## SPINACH AND BLUEBERRY COLLAGEN SMOOTHIE

Ingredients

- 1 Cup Fresh Spinach

- ½ Cup Frozen Blueberries

- ½ Cup Other Frozen Berries Such as strawberries or raspberries

- 1 Tbsp Almond Butter Or peanut butter

- 1 Cup Vanilla Almond Milk Or other nut

  milk

- 1 Scoop Marine Collagen

Instructions

- Add your ingredients, in order above, into

  your blender. Adding the spinach in first

  insures it gets well-blended.

- Blend until smooth, adding additional

  almond milk as needed to reach the

  desired consistency.

# STRAWBERRY MANGO BANANA SMOOTHIE

## INGREDIENTS

- 1 cup dairy free milk coconut milk for AIP & SCD

- handful frozen strawberries

- handful frozen mango

- 1/2 frozen banana

- 2 scoops collagen peptides

## INSTRUCTIONS

- Add all of the ingredients to a blender/nutribullet

- Blend until smooth, and enjoy!

- *Optional: blend in spinach, kale, or any other greens.

- *To make the smoothie more like banana "nice" cream, use a whole frozen banana or add more frozen mango and strawberries.

## CREAMY STRAWBERRY TAHINI COLLAGEN SMOOTHIE

### Ingredients

- 1 1/2 cups almond milk or any other dairy free milk, coconut water or filtered tap water

- 1 Tbsp tahini

- 1 cup spinach

- 1/2 cup strawberries

- 1 banana frozen, chopped

- 3 dates whole, pitted

- 1 scoop Vanilla Collagen Peptides

- Pinch of cinnamon

## Directions

- Combine all ingredients in blender. Blend until smooth.

## GREEN BREAKFAST SMOOTHIE WITH COLLAGEN

### Ingredients

- 1 cup frozen mixed berries

- 2 handfuls baby spinach (or any triple-washed organic leafy greens)

- 1/4 avocado

- 1 cup your favorite unsweetened coconut or nut milk

- 1 tbsp almond butter

- 1 scoop Natural Force Organic Vanilla Whey Protein

- 1 scoop Natural Force Collagen Peptides (omit if vegetarian)

- 2-3 ice cubes

Instructions

- Layer the ingredients in your blender by adding nut milk first, then berries, greens, avocado, almond butter, Whey Protein,

Collagen Peptides, and finally the ice and spinach.

- Blend until smooth, adding additional nut milk if a thinner consistency is desired.

- Pour into your favorite cup and enjoy! For maximum nutrient content, drink smoothie immediately.

**Recipe Notes**

Variations

- For more sweetness: Add 1 small banana or 2-3 dates

- For more fiber: Add 1-2 tsps chia seeds or flax seeds

- For more healthy fat: Add a tbsp of Organic MCT Oil

- For dairy-free: Use 1 scoop of Natural Force Organic Plant Protein in place of Natural Force Organic Whey Protein Concentrate

# CREATIVE ENERGY-BOOSTING COLLAGEN AND COCOA SMOOTHIES

## INGREDIENTS

**PINEAPPLE TASTE:**

- 2 cups cubed fresh pineapple

- 1/2 lemon, peeled

- 1 tablespoon organic Cocoa Powder

- 1 tablespoon unflavored gelatin powder

- 1 package orange flavored vitamin C powder (0.3 oz) (optional)

- 1/2 cup pea milk or almond milk

- 2 cups of water

**COFFEE TASTE:**

- 1 cup coffee, freshly brewed

- 1 tablespoon organic Cocoa Powder

- 1 tablespoon unflavored gelatin powder

- 1/2 cup pea milk or almond milk

- 2 drops liquid stevia (or more to taste)

- 4 leaves of fresh chocolate mint (optional)

INSTRUCTIONS

**PINEAPPLE TASTE:**

- Blend everything in a high-speed blender (like a Vitamix) until frothy and smooth. Enjoy immediately.

**COFFEE TASTE:**

- Place all ingredients, except the coffee into a high-speed blender. Pour the hot coffee into a cup, allowing some of the hot steam to release. Then transfer the coffee also into the high-speed blender. Blend everything until frothy and smooth. Enjoy immediately!

# BLUEBERRY KEFIR LEMON COLLAGEN SMOOTHIE

## Ingredients

- 1 cup Blueberry Lowfat Kefir

- ½ cup frozen blueberries

- 2 scoops Further Foods Collagen Peptidesn Peptides

- 1 tbsp lemon juice

- 1 tsp freshly grated lemon zest

## Directions

- Add all ingredients to the pitcher of a high-powered blender.

- Blend on high until smooth, or until desired consistency is reached.

# DAILY COLLAGEN BEAUTY SMOOTHIE

## Ingredients

- 1 scoop Ancestral Nutrition Collagen Protein + Super Greens

- 1-2 kale leaves

- 1 tbsp chia seeds

- 1/2 cup mixed berries (or blueberries, strawberries, etc.)

- 1/2 avocado

- 1/2 cup water

- 1/2 cup yogurt or kefir (dairy-free or grass-fed/full fat)

## Instructions

- Add everything to a high speed blender and blend until smooth!

## KETO COLLAGEN PUMPKIN SPICE SMOOTHIE

### Ingredients

- 2 ice cubes

- 8 oz unsweetened almond milk

- 2 tablespoons almond butter

- 1 scoop Keto Perfect Keto Chocolate Collagen Powder

- pinch of pumpkin pie spice

### Instructions

- Mix everything in a smoothie/blender cup and blend for 20-30 seconds.

- Enjoy immediate

# ENERGY GREEN COLLAGEN SMOOTHIE

Ingredients

- ½ banana

- ¼ avocado

- 1 handful fresh kale

- 1 tbsp chia seeds

- 1 tbsp maple syrup

- 1 scoop Vanilla Coconut Collagen Fuel

- 1-2 handfuls ice

- toppings: roasted coconut chips and
  additional chia seeds

- Add all ingredients to a high powered blender and blend until smooth.

- Transfer to a bowl, add toppings and enjoy!

## GREEN GINGER COLLAGEN SMOOTHIE

### INGREDIENTS

- 1 1/2 cups baby spinach (35 grams)

- 2/3 cup light coconut milk, frozen into cubes (150 grams)

- 1 medium green apple, chopped (220 grams)

- 1 small banana, sliced and frozen (78 grams)

- 1/2 large mango, chopped (132 grams)

- 3 scoops Sports Research Grass-Fed
  Collagen Peptides

- Enough ginger beer to blend to desired
  consistency

INSTRUCTIONS

- Add all ingredients to a blender, then
  blend until smoothies reach desired
  consistency.  Add more ginger beer if
  needed.

# NEOCELL STRAWBERRY COLLAGEN SMOOTHIE

## INGREDIENTS

- 2 cups coconut water

- 1 cup mixed berries strawberry, blackberry, blueberry

- 2 tablespoons Neocell Super Collagen Powder

- Handful of goji berries

- 1 banana

- ½ apple

- juice of ½ lemon

- 1 teaspoon chia seeds

## INSTRUCTIONS

- Blend and glow.

# CREAMY MANGO COLLAGEN SMOOTHIE

Ingredients

- 1/2 cup unsweetened yogurt tangy not sweet

- 3/4-1 cup frozen mango chunks organic

- 1 tbsp chia seeds

- 1 scoop unflavored collagen powder I like Vital Proteins

- 1/2 cup unsweetened coconut milk

- 1-2 tbsp additional unsweetened coconut milk optional

- 1-2 cups ice

- In a highspeed blender, blast the mango and coconut milk till well blended.

- Add all ingredients except the ice.  Blast until blended, again.

- For extra creaminess add a blended smoothie to the freezer for 1/2 hour.

- Sprinkle on all your toppings and dive in via straw OR spoon - Your choice.

## BLUEBERRY ACAI GREEN SMOOTHIE WITH COLLAGEN (DAIRY-FREE)

### INGREDIENTS

- 1 cup frozen wild, organic blueberries

- 1 frozen banana

- 2 cups organic spinach

- 1 tablespoon organic acai powder

- 2 tablespoons collagen protein

- 2 tablespoons organic chia seeds

- 1.5 cups unsweetened almond milk


INSTRUCTIONS

- Add all ingredients to a blender and blend

  until smooth. Serve immediately

## GOLDEN GLOW SMOOTHIE

Ingredients:

- ½ cup full-fat coconut milk

- ¼ cup collagen peptides

- ½ teaspoon turmeric powder

- Pinch of freshly ground pepper

- 1 small frozen banana, cut into coins

- 1 Persian or Armenian seedless cucumber
  (6-inches), cut into coins

- 1 cup frozen mango chunks

- Honey, maple syrup, or stevia to taste
  (optional)

Method:

- Grab your blender and pour in the
  coconut milk, collagen peptides,
  turmeric…

- Blitz until smooth

- Divide into two cups or drink it all up
  yourself

# COLLAGEN PEANUT BUTTER SMOOTHIE

## Ingredients

- 1 small frozen banana

- 2 tbsp peanut butter

- 1 scoop of Vital Proteins Collagen Peptides (unflavored)

- 1 tbsp chia seeds

- 1 tsp cinnamon

- 1 cup almond milk

## Instructions

- Add all ingredients into a high power blender

- Blend and enjoy ice cold!

- Use pre-cut frozen pieces of banana and you won't have to add ice.

## BLUE-APPLE AND COLLAGEN PEPTIDE SMOOTHIE

Ingredients

- 2 cups Coconut Water

- 1/4 cup Blueberries Organic (fresh or frozen)

- 1/4 cup Pineapple Organic (fresh or frozen)

- 2 scoops Collagen Peptides Use only grass-fed for best results

- In a blender, mix together the coconut water, blueberries and pineapple until smooth

- Add the collagen peptides powder and pulse in blender until fully mixed

- Garnish with lime slice (optional).

## PINEAPPLE BANANA PROTEIN SMOOTHIE

### INGREDIENTS

- 1 Cup Vanilla Almond Milk

- 2 Scoops Perfect Hydrolyzed Collagen

- 1 Cup Pineapple Chunks

- 1 Banana

- 1/2 Cup Ice



- Combine all ingredients in blender and

blend until smooth. Enjoy immediately or

store in refrigerator for up to one hour.



- If you don't have collagen powder on

hand, you can substitute it with a serving

of vanilla protein powder or 1/2 cup plain

Greek yogurt.

www.ingramcontent.com/pod-product-compliance
Lightning Source LLC
Chambersburg PA
CBHW052127150726

48002CB00006B/2506